Ya-Vo
(The Hidden Path)

SIVASANKAR S.J.
TRANSLATED BY - PADMA AMARNAATH

INDIA • SINGAPORE • MALAYSIA

Copyright © Padma Amarnaath 2024
All Rights Reserved.

ISBN 979-8-89415-340-7

Contents

Contents

Contents

Contents

Foreword

While I was reading some philosophical texts along with, I got very fond of SUFI & ZEN texts. As a writer and basically a reader I was really surprised to know that in this Age-old Tamil tradition there are no collective philosophical stories at all. All the stories we know are THENALIRAMAN, BIRBAL, MARIYAATHAI RAMAN, MULLA, HODJA, AESOP, PANCHATHANTHIRA which are not of Tamil origin and I found that most of the fables, parables, legends myths, and folklores were not native too. When aside I thought of the long back discourse tradition of the Tamils I found a master and student I christened them ya-o (**yaavum-ontru** one who considers everything same) and the student ya-a (**yaarum atravan** one who has no one) in a dialectical way the names are pronounced ya-vo & ya-vaa. And that is the history. I then wrote 108 fictious dialogues, 108 being a folk tradition with mundane and philosophical touch. When I thought of the genre of the stories I again christened it a new term as "OCCULT FICTION". Thus so far a sequel is also written. The trilogy part is now on progress.

Smt. Padma a personality introduced by my buddy brother JP, was very much interested in the text. She first translated the sequels which were very fine and adorable. As a translator myself I wondered how she translated the southern dialects which much ease and clarity. After that being a motivational speaker she wrote elucidations for the discourses in a motivational perspective. Long before commentaries for books happened in a variety of perspectives. I'm happy that such a translation with commentary has happened for my book too. I thank Smt. Padma for this venture and for being a great friend. Hope the readers will enjoy the experience

Regards

Sivasankar .s .j
prismshivaezhil@gmail.com

Author Note

Today, we often hear Zen stories from China or Japan, but Tamil Nadu, our own culturally rich land, also has its share of Zen tales. In ancient India, wisdom was passed down through conversations between teachers and students in the Gurukula system until the thirteenth century. What if Thiruvalluvar, the sage of Thirukkural, had answered questions in a philosophical dialogue with students? Imagine a student asking a question, and Thiruvalluvar responding with wise verses. Whereupon, Thirukkural only has Thiruvalluvar's responses; the students' voices are hidden, adding an intriguing aspect to this ancient conversation.

Locations like homes, temples, workplaces, and outdoor spaces such as open halls and shaded areas were hubs for discussions. In the Tamil philosophical tradition, numerous dialogues between teachers and students have vanished over time.

Introducing "Ya - Vo," a book seamlessly extending the ancient tradition of the (Master - disciple) Gurukula system.

This book blends religious, philosophical, and a touch of active politics, depicting reactions against inequality and proactive involvement. It's crucial to understand that the entire story is a creation from beginning to end.

What distinguishes this book from the traditional storytelling format is, its capacity to transform reading into a participatory experience. It encourages readers to think, reflect and in some instances, respond to the questions woven into the narrative, fostering a sense of active engagement.

I am over joyed to have translated this Tamil book to English, which belongs to a distinct genre. This book resonates with the language and lifestyle of ancient scriptures. The activities involving Ya-vaa and his Master Ya-vo, offer a glimpse into the lifestyle patterns of our ancient times.

It is a genuine honor to translate this remarkable masterpiece crafted by Thiru SivaShankar. In this work, certain nuances of ancient Tamil literary texts are decoded into a simple question-and-answer format. As I immerse myself in the pages of this work, I feel a profound sense of privilege in presenting the encapsulated wisdom by providing an explanation below each chapter. It was indeed author Thiru. SivaShankar who requested that I elucidate the chapters from my perspective. I have endeavored to meticulously extract and serve the pearls of wisdom from each chapter, ready to be savored.

Additionally, readers can explore their wisdom and note down their explanations in the given lines below each chapter. Let's dive into this fascinating philosophical journey together and explore to learn more.

Evolve, Encourage, Empower.

Padma Amarnaath

Thank you.

1.

Shadow

Master Yavo patiently sat down for a refreshing oil massage, followed by a warm bath.

Student Yavaa gently sat beside, with apprehension surfacing.

"Master, I am scared."

"When and for what, Yavaa?"

"Always, and for everything. It lingers within me," Yavaa confessed.

"That's your shadow. It accompanies you. Just as a cow fears the shadow of a whip, or a horse fears its own shadow. Haven't you heard of this?" enquired the Master.

"Hmm. Is fear inherently good or bad?" the student asked, seeking clarity.

"A knife's shadow can pierce, a stick's shadow can strike. Isn't that agonizing, Yavaa?" the Master elucidated.

"How can I rid myself of this fear, Master?"

"By avoiding shadows," the Master suggested.

"But how?" he pressed for more guidance.

"Stay away from light," the Master concluded.

—'Stay away from Light' here means, shedding light on your ignorance and your suppressed feelings.

2.

'I'

"Master, when will ' I ' cease to exist?" Yavaa inquired.

"Emulate the nature of a dog," the Master advised. "It is the sole path to subdue the ego. But Yavaa, a wagging tail and licking tongue are symbolic acts of submission and are not inherent aspects of one's being" explained the Master.

—I see the Master's advice to "emulate the nature of a dog", as a technique of adopting qualities such as loyalty, simplicity, and unconditional love. These traits help a person to get rid of their selfish nature. Dogs wag their tails and lick their tongues to show they're friendly and willing to follow or obey others. The Master further clarifies that, such symbolic acts of submission, are not inherently a part of human nature. Humans use gestures like smiling or nodding to show respect and get along with others. But just copying these actions without truly understanding humility and selflessness, won't help someone get rid of their ego. It's important to genuinely embrace these qualities from within.

Additionally, the answer highlights the importance of learning from nature and observing simple yet profound lessons that animals can teach us about life.

3.

The Rudder

In preparation for a household ceremony, new pots were being ordered.

The Master had ventured to the market for this purpose, and student Yavaa accompanied him.

"The wheels alleviate the burden, Yavaa. A positive attitude serves as the wheel of life," the Master declared, moving gracefully through the market.

—The Master's statement about a positive attitude serving as the "wheel of life" is a clear psychological perspective.

Cognitive-behavioral theory states that our thoughts, feelings, and behaviors are interconnected. A positive attitude can influence our thoughts, leading to more optimistic perceptions of challenges and setbacks. This, in turn, can affect our emotions positively and motivate us to take constructive actions.

Positive psychology focuses on strengths, virtues, and factors that contribute to a fulfilling life. This enhances our well-being, and improvises interpersonal relationships.

4.

Relationship

Master carefully emptied the cow dung pit from within, passing the contents to Yavaa, who stood at the pit's opening.

Yavaa then disposed of the dung in the nearby fields before returning for the next batch.

Once the task was complete, they cleansed their hands and settled down for a meal.

"After budding and flourishing, does not all eventually transform into dryness that disappoints, Master?" Yavaa inquired.

"Indeed, my child, it's not solely the nature of the soil alone," the Master responded.

—In this conversation, Yavaa discusses how things go through stages of growth and decline, using terms like 'budding' and 'flourishing'. It's not just about plants; it applies to people and their relationships too. Just like plants, people and their relationships have times of growth and prosperity, as well as times of struggle. The Master emphasizes that relationships aren't solely influenced by external factors, like the soil, but also by internal factors, such as our thoughts and feelings.

The Master stresses the importance of understanding life's natural ups and downs. Accepting this reality can improve our mental well-being and help us find inner peace, rather than feeling disappointed or dried up (as Yavaa had mentioned).

5.

"Silence"

During a tranquil evening, basking in the refreshing breeze beneath the neem tree, Student Yavaa posed a question, "Master, is there a correlation between the tranquility of the mind and age?"

"One can discover serenity under the glaring sun and turmoil within the shade, Yavaa," the Master promptly replied.

—This metaphor is great and easy to understand. Finding serenity under the glaring sun and turmoil within the shade suggests that, one can feel peaceful even when things are tough, or feel troubled, even when everything seems fine. How one feels inside is more important than what's happening around. For example, sometimes young, passionate people stay calm in tough times, while older people, who have more experience, might feel upset for no reason. This shows that feeling calm isn't always about external factors like age, experience or what's happening outside.

Staying calm is purely a choice.

6.

Persistence

Master Yavo was enjoying playful moments with his grandchildren when he noticed Yavaa approaching him.

Upon nearing, the troubled student expressed, "Thoughts are tormenting, Master."

In response, the Master recounted a tale, "Once, a frog tumbled into a pot of milk. Undeterred, it persistently swam across the pot. Eventually, the milk churned and transformed into butter, allowing the frog to effortlessly leap out from it."

—The story subtly suggests to Yavaa that he should release his burden by actively working on it, rather than worrying. It illustrates the psychological principle of perseverance and adaptation in the face of challenges. The frog, initially finding itself in a difficult situation, doesn't give up. Swimming across the pot symbolizes resilience and determination.

As the frog continues to swim, the milk churns and transforms into butter. This transformation represents the potential for individuals who persist and continue to make efforts to often find unexpected solutions or opportunities for improvement.

7.

Complexities

During an evening puppet show, the Master sat absorbed in the performance.

Yavaa, equally enthralled, exclaimed, "Puppets... puppets..." in excitement.

Gradually, he turned to his Master and asked, "Master, are sorrow, crisis, and turmoil the same all over the universe?"

"Much like a fish lured by a worm, despite being tethered to a hook, individuals get drawn towards committing sins and grave errors," the Master replied.

—The Master's analogy suggests that the root cause for suffering, is temptation. People are often enticed by temptation, even when they know it may lead to negative consequences. The immediate pleasure or perceived benefit from committing the action can overshadow long-term consequences. This is similar to the fish being lured by the worm's promise of food.

On the other hand, there is a psychology behind individuals being drawn towards committing sins despite knowing the potential consequences. The phenomenon behind is complex, involving various cognitive, emotional, and social factors. In Fyodor Dostoevsky's "Crime and Punishment," the protagonist Raskolnikov commits murder, believing it is justified for the greater good. His internal struggle and rationalizations provide a deep exploration of moral psychology.

8.

Talent

Master Yavo was tending to his hens, feeling the gentle breeze and the warmth of the summer sun, which lulled him into a brief nap.

Startled from his slumber, he opened his eyes to witness an eagle soaring above the sky.

With a knowing look, Master Yavo murmured, "Fear is the power of the snake."

With that, he gathered his hens and made his way back home.

—Fear can be as strong as a scary snake. Snake here represents the situation. This fear influences a person's behavior, leading them to avoid places where snakes might be present or to experience intense anxiety in such situations.

Just as a snake's power lies in its ability to instill fear, the person's fear holds significant power over his behavior and psychological well-being. This fear becomes our obstruction adds power to the challenge (snake).

9.

Maturity

Master Yavo was observing the trees on his farm when he noticed his student Yavaa approaching.

"I often find myself overwhelmed by emotions, Master. I struggle to maintain control," Yavaa confessed.

"It's only natural, Yavaa," the Master reassured before continuing his analogy. "In their unripe state, grapes may taste sour. Once fully ripened, they become sweet. However, when soaked and fermented, they turn bitter. Each phase of life carries its unique flavor."

—This statement suggests that different stages of life can have varying experiences, just like grapes that go through different phases of taste.

Think about a person's journey through education. At first, it might be tough, just like sour grapes. But as you learn and grow, it gets sweeter, like ripe grapes. When you become an adult, you face new challenges, which can be like sour grapes again. Our thinking patterns evolve throughout life, from concrete thinking in childhood to abstract reasoning in adulthood, affecting our perception of experiences.

But even though life has ups and downs, each part of it helps you grow and learn, making your journey unique and flavorful. Life has different phases, each with its own experiences and emotions.

Enjoy the journey.

10.

One Word

As Yavaa savored the slices of wild jackfruit, he posed a question to his Master, "Do words hold such immense significance?"

"A solitary word planted in your heart is akin to a banyan tree within a seed. To live in accordance with just one word would necessitate more than a lifetime, Yavaa," the Master replied.

—The Master's statement suggests that a single word, when deeply rooted within someone, can have profound and expansive implications.

For example, consider the word "compassion." If someone truly internalizes and embodies this word, it can shape every aspect of his life. He will start to reflect kindness and empathy towards others.

However, fully living in accordance with the principle of compassion, would involve a lifetime of continuous learning, growth, and practice. It would require consistently making compassionate choices and actions in various situations. Living in alignment with just that one word would require more than a single lifetime.

11.

To Give Birth

On that day, Master Yavo was fasting, while his student was starving.

Master Yavo observed his hungry student, Yavaa.

Noticing the exhaustion, he remarked, "A dog that leads the sightless man can also chase a blind man. Such is the nature of money."

—The analogy highlights the inherent duality of money and one's socioeconomic status. It can be a force for good or for harm, depending on how it is used and perceived.

For example, the two individuals here, one wealthy and the other impoverished, both are experiencing hunger. The wealthy person, represented by "a dog that leads the sightless man," may choose to abstain from food voluntarily, perceiving it as a form of self-discipline or spiritual practice. In contrast, the impoverished person, symbolised by 'blind man', lacks the resources to obtain food, experiencing hunger (lack of money) chasing him.

12.

Mothers Love

While engrossed in preparing the electuary for sustaining youthfulness, Master Yavo paused in silence to contemplate his student Yava's question.

"Can the love of a mother be measured in terms of distance, Master?" inquired Yavaa.

"It's akin to the distance between a tamarind tree and a neem tree, Yavaa," the Master responded.

—The Master's response suggests that the love of a mother cannot be measured in conventional terms, such as physical distance. Instead, he uses the metaphor of the distance between a tamarind tree and a neem tree.

Tamarind and neem trees are often found growing in close proximity to each other in certain regions. However, despite their physical closeness, they are distinct and separate entities with different characteristics.

The tamarind tree is associated with a tangy sweetness, representing the joys and pleasures experienced in the relationship between a child and its mother. On the other hand, the neem tree is characterized by its bitterness, symbolizing the challenges and sacrifices inherent in maternal love. Despite its bitter taste, the neem tree is valued for its medicinal properties and benefits, highlighting the depth and selflessness of a mother's love.

13.

Speed

"In the uncharted terrain, when you anticipate the obstacles ahead, you assume the role of a bat. Yet, when you wait, allowing time to unveil the path, you become a snail, Yavaa. The tiger bears stripes and a deer bears spots. Here, by nature, the prey itself flees to evade capture. In the forest, there exists neither a winning nor a losing scenario."

—A bat estimating obstacles ahead and adapting flight paths reflects proactive decision-making, where one can anticipate challenges and plan accordingly. On the contrary, waiting for the path to clear, represents a more cautious approach, prioritizing safety over speed or progress, where we become a snail.

Both the tiger and deer have spots, but their behaviors and survival strategies differ based on their risk assessments and capabilities. The tiger takes calculated risks in hunting, while the deer relies on speed and agility to evade predators.

"The Tortoise and the Hare," story reminds us of the slow and steady approach of the tortoise (similar to the snail), who wins the race against the overconfident hare (akin to the bat). Whether we humans prioritize speed or caution, or balance different strategies, each approach has its merits and limitations.

In the forest (world), there's no clear winner or loser.

14.

To Walk Out

The Master engaged in conversation with several individuals on the veranda, but one by one, they departed, leaving only Yavaa behind.

"I find myself uninterested in everything," Yavaa lamented.

"Oh, is that so? In that case, you may also leave the place. However, remember to close the door on your way out, for that is how I too walked out," the Master replied.

—I clearly see this message as a reminder for the choices made and accountability in one's life. Imagine someone who feels bored with his job, hobbies, and relationships. They might not feel excited and might think about leaving everything behind to find something more exciting. Yava's statement "I find myself uninterested in everything" suggests an existential crisis—a deep questioning of one's purpose, values, and the meaning of life.

The Master's advice to "close the door on your way out" may symbolize letting go of past attachments, regrets, or negative emotions to move forward.

Siddhartha embarks on a spiritual journey to find meaning and purpose, facing similar existential questions as Yavaa, who later becomes world renowned Buddha. Existential psychology focuses on understanding life's big questions like meaning and purpose. It often looks at how philosophical and spiritual ideas influence our thoughts and feelings about life.

15.

Strange

Engaged in etching a stone slab, student Yavaa queried his Master with a sense of wonder, "Isn't the mind an enigmatic entity, Master?"

"It truly is. It both discerns and selects," replied the Master.

"In that case, will I be afflicted by a mental disorder, Master?" inquired Yava.

"The mind itself is a disorder," stated Master Yavo.

—Imagine someone going shopping for a special occasion, like a wedding. As they browse through various clothing options, their mind discerns the style, color, and fit that would be most suitable for the event. They use their mind to carefully select outfits.

However, amidst the excitement of shopping, their mind also experiences moments of disorder. They may feel overwhelmed by the multitude of choices available, leading to indecision and uncertainty.

This answer emphasises that disorderliness is a fundamental aspect of mind's nature, and humans really need not get worried about 'mental disorder'. Mind, many a times, jumps and acts like a monkey.

16.

Comfort

In the early morning, they journeyed to the river bank to gather fertile soil.

During their return, Yavaa inquired, "Is there anything more virtuous than giving religious scriptures, clothing, and medicines?"

"A helping hand in times of need, Yavaa," swiftly replied the Master.

—The students psychology of social exchange suggests that people give and help others expecting some form of reciprocity, whether emotional, social, or material. The Master's emphasis on selfless giving without expecting anything in return, challenges this traditional view, promoting altruism and compassion as virtues in themselves.

17.

Melting

Master Yavo visited student Yavaa's hut, who had been absent for a while.

Master was sad to see him in a debilitated state with sunken and darkened eyes.

"I had cautioned you about the perils of unwanted thoughts, Yavaa. They act like fire and our body is akin to a structure of wax. Do you understand?" the Master reminded him.

—There is always a danger of thinking too much and brooding over negative thoughts. These thoughts act like fire to our wax-like bodies. Negative thoughts slowly harm our confidence and mental health.

For instance, imagine someone who often feels insecure and compares themselves to others. It's definitely a fire, burning away their self-esteem. The thoughts we focus on and how we feel about ourselves, matter a lot.

18.

Excess

Master Yavo stoked the fire fervently, his eyes ablaze, attempting to intensify the flames. Curiously, student Yavaa asked, "If hatred is deemed the antithesis of love, what embodies the pinnacle of love?"

"Amidst physical intimacy on one end and profound emptiness on the other, love, can only echo love," the Master responded.

Student Yavaa, moved by his Master's words, gently brought the Master's hand to his eyes in a gesture of prayer.

—This answer explains love, intimacy, and profound emptiness. If hatred is seen as the antithesis of love, the pinnacle of love could be described as unconditional love or altruistic love. Unconditional love is a selfless, enduring affection and care for another person without expecting anything in return. It transcends physical attraction or fleeting emotions and is often characterized by empathy, compassion, and understanding.

Consider a couple deeply in love. They may experience moments of intense physical intimacy, symbolizing their affection and desire for each other. Conversely, they may also encounter times of emotional distance or emptiness, where external factors or conflicts temporarily disrupt their connection.

However, even during challenging times, their love echoes and reverberates through their acts of kindness, support, and understanding. This supports the Masters explanation that, true love can only echo love.

19.

Indifference

"In discerning, comprehending, observing, and unraveling, what kind of challenges do we encounter, Master?" inquired Yavaa.

"Waterfalls, cuckoos, the sky, flowers, and the air, can you truly know or understand them? Can you decipher or truly see them? The complexity lies within the words, Yavaa.... merely words." responded the Master.

—There is always an inherent challenge of understanding and comprehending the complexities of life and existence.

By mentioning elements of nature such as waterfalls, cuckoos, the sky, flowers, and the air, the Master is highlighting the vastness and intricacy of the world around us.

For example, consider a waterfall. We can observe its majestic beauty and hear the soothing sound of its cascading water. But, understanding its ecological significance, geological formation, and impact on its surrounding environment, requires deep knowledge and insight.

Similarly, the sky. From the patterns of the stars to the intricacies of weather systems, there is much about the sky that remains mysterious and beyond our complete comprehension.

In essence, the Master is suggesting that despite our efforts to discern, comprehend, observe, and unravel the complexities of life and nature, there are inherent limitations to our understanding. Mere linguistic descriptions may not capture the full depth and intricacy of these phenomena.

I see this answer highlighting the humility and respect we should have for the mysteries of the world.

20.

Guide

In a delightful season, during the early hours, "What did your Master teach you, Master?" Yavaa softly inquired.

The Master responded, "There is no suffering in treading a path that has no path. There is no goal in following a trail that is formless. Where there is no endpoint, there is no voyage. There is no guidance in a space void of teachings."

—Don't worry about the destination. Rather, enjoy the journey. Master's response revolves around the concept of purpose and direction in life.

When the Master mentions "no suffering in treading a path that has no path," he suggests that the absence of a predefined path can alleviate the burden of expectations and pressures.

For example, we find many people around us, overwhelmed by societal expectations and the pressure to pursue a specific career or lifestyle. Rather, they may discover a sense of freedom and authenticity in navigating their own journey, regardless of societal norms or expectations.

Similarly, when the Master speaks of "no goal in following a trail that is formless," he suggests that without a clear objective or endpoint, the journey loses its purpose and meaning. This highlights the importance of having goals and aspirations to guide our actions and decisions in life.

Overall, the Master's teachings emphasizes the importance of finding purpose and direction in life, while also acknowledging the value of embracing uncertainty and forging one's own path. It encourages individuals to seek fulfillment not only in reaching goals but also in the journey itself.

21.

Possessions

Engrossed in tending to the soil in his backyard, Student Yavaa engaged in conversations about worldly affairs, including discussions about kings and rulers.

As the discussion drew to a close, Yavaa posed a question to his Master, "Does conquering and ruling the world mean seizing nations and claiming lands?"

"There isn't a single individual who has truly conquered even a tiny grain of sand, Yavaa," the Master replied.

—The Master's response reflects a profound understanding of the human psyche and the limitations of human power. It highlights the inherent inability of humans to exert absolute control over creation and nature.

From a philosophical standpoint, even the smallest element, like a grain of sand, which is part of a larger creation, transcends human influence. While humans may possess the ability to shape and manipulate the environment to some extent, we are ultimately subject to the forces of nature and the universe.

This perspective underscores humility and also acknowledges the transitory nature of human existence.

22.

Vision

On a serene morning, Master Yavo strode briskly along the riverbank while his student Yavaa arrived to attend to his morning duties.

Observing the situation, the Master remained silent, not wishing to interrupt.

"Are you observing or perceiving me, Master?" inquired Yavaa.

"Observing and perceiving differ as greatly as a mountain, Yavaa. Yet, I find myself fallen within my own gaze," the Master replied.

—Observation typically involves the act of simply witnessing or noticing, while perception involves interpreting and making meaning out of those observations based on one's subjective experiences, beliefs, and biases.

The Master says that he is "fallen within his own gaze", implying that his perception of the world is inevitably influenced by his own thoughts, emotions, and beliefs.

Let me make it simple. Imagine a person observing a crowded street. He may notice the hustle and bustle of people going about their daily lives, the sounds of traffic and the various sights and smells of the environment. However, each one's perception of the scene may be colored by their own past experiences, cultural background, and personal biases. One same street, can look either chaotic or vibrant.

Observation and perception are subjective nature of human experience and our inherent biases shape our understanding of reality.

23.

Truth

On that particular day, Master Yavo appeared remarkably joyous.

A countenance that typically graced the world with a simple smile, now radiated with laughter.

Curious, Yavaa inquired, "What is the source of your happiness today, Master?"

"I have discovered a profound truth, Yavaa. To utter falsehood, there is no need for a tongue" the Master replied.

—As we all know, a person who finds happiness in being true to themselves and others, prioritize honesty. They openly express their thoughts and feelings without resorting to lies or deception, thus cultivating lasting happiness and fulfillment in their lives. The phrase "To utter falsehood, there is no need for a tongue" suggests that lies or deceit don't always require verbal expression; they can manifest in actions, thoughts, or omissions as well.

However, humans, sometimes choose to utter falsehoods due to various reasons such as fear, desire for personal gain, or social pressure.

24.

Quest

Engaged in the task of drawing water from the well, Student Yavaa, was toiling hard with the aid of water baskets suspended from his shoulders.

Meanwhile, the Master passed by, making his way towards the fields. Later, as they shared their morning porridge together, they engaged in conversation.

"When the pursuit or search surpasses its limits, what befalls humanity, Master?" Yavaa inquired.

"It's quite straightforward and simple Yavaa. Everything becomes simple. Thirst seeks water, just as the well seeks thirst," the Master replied.

—The pursuit or search for something often fuels human motivation and actions. When this pursuit surpasses its limits, it can lead to an obsession or imbalance. The initial desire becomes all-consuming, overshadowing other aspects of life.

When we focus on one thing, life gets simpler because the focus narrows down to this singular goal or desire. Just like when we are really thirsty, we just want water. And when we want something, we will find a way to get it, like a well always has water for those who need it.

Basically, it means that when you keep things simple and don't obsess over stuff, you'll find what you're looking for more easily. It's important to know when to stop and not make things too complicated.

25.

We Become the Answer

"Why are there a lot of questions without answers? Why so many hidden calculations and ideas? Why is the world so complicated and odd?" Yavaa asked.

"Answers can come from the questions themselves, Yavaa. We can ask questions that fit our own answers. When the Universe seems to be a question, we become the answer. When we become the question, the Universe becomes the answer," the Master explained.

—Never forget the power of questioning, in shaping our reality and understanding of the world around us. Humans often frame their experiences and perceptions through questions. By becoming the question or the answer, we take an active role in shaping our reality and relationship with the Universe.

For example, imagine someone who believes they are unworthy of love. They may ask themselves questions like, "Why am I always alone?" or "What's wrong with me?" These questions reinforce their negative beliefs, leading to a sense of inadequacy.

However, if they start asking themselves questions like, "What qualities do I have that make me deserving of love?" or "How can I improve my relationships?" they begin to shift their perspective. By asking more empowering questions, they open themselves up to new possibilities and insights.

Similarly, when faced with challenges or uncertainties in life, the questions we ask ourselves can influence how we perceive and respond to them. By asking constructive and introspective questions, we can gain deeper insights and navigate life's complexities with greater clarity and purpose.

26.

God

Truly, who is God?" Yavaa asked, feeling exasperated.

"Sleep, hunger, sex, fear, anger, and animosity are all bodily responses, correct? This instinctive aspect of our being is God. Furthermore, for a blind individual, the light that remains unseen becomes God," Master Yavo patiently explained.

—The fundamental bodily instincts, inherent in every human being, are seen as expressions of God's presence within us. Additionally, for someone who is blind and cannot perceive light, the unseen light takes on a symbolic representation of the divine. It suggests that even what is hidden or imperceptible to the senses can embody the essence of divinity.

Master's explanation gives a holistic understanding of spirituality, suggesting that the divine can be found in both the tangible and intangible, the seen and the unseen, within and beyond human perception.

27.

To Experience

Engaged in the quiet task of sorting and dyeing threads, Master Yavo was approached by Student Yavaa with a question. "Do we initially perceive sensations through our senses, which later accumulate as our experiences, or are experiences and sensory perceptions unrelated?" inquired Yavaa.

Emerging from his silence, Master Yavo replied, "Light is an experience. We don't perceive light through our eyes."

—While sensory perceptions provide the raw data, our experiences are shaped by how we interpret, integrate, and assign meaning to this data.

Imagine a warm glow of sunlight on a summer day, which can evoke feelings of happiness and warmth, or the eerie atmosphere created by moonlight on a foggy night, which can evoke a sense of mystery and unease. In essence, the statement proposes that our experience of light encompasses not only what we see but also how we feel and interpret it.

28.

Togetherness

"The Universe is interconnected. How do you perceive it? Well, how do you describe it?" Yavaa stood silently, unsure.

Master Yavo elucidated, "Coolness combined with water, the aroma within a flower, the inherent luminosity of heat—what do you believe these aspects to be?

—The philosophy of interconnectedness emphasizes the idea that everything in the universe is interconnected and interdependent. It suggests that all phenomena, from the smallest particle to the grandest cosmic event, are intimately linked and influence each other in intricate ways.

Despite this, some individuals choose to isolate themselves and live as islands (just saying).

29.

Wavering Mind

Amidst the onset of the winter season, the Master and the student took a moment to relax. They sat down, applying fresh butter on their chapped lips.

"From the very start, seeds of distrust and skepticism have been sown among humanity. Why is this so, Master?" inquired Yava.

"They serve as coverings. Truth emerges veiled in disbelief, while doubtfulness appears shrouded in truth" replied the Master.

—The commencement of this chapter was captivating as it depicted a scene where a Master and student were seen applying butter to chapped lips. Such narrative elements evoke a sense of nostalgia, reminding us of age-old traditional methods and practices.

Truth is often complex and multifaceted, making it difficult to grasp fully. When truth is presented, it may be met with disbelief because it challenges existing beliefs, assumptions, or perceptions. What appears as truth to one person may seem doubtful or false to another, highlighting the subjective nature of truth and the role of personal bias in shaping our perceptions.

Apparently, truth hides all uncertainties.

30.

Praising

"Shouldn't a preacher focus only on preaching, and not engage himself in other matters, Master?" Yavaa asked, looking confused.

Master Yavo stood silently, smiling at him. Yavaa repeated his question.

"Trickery is often admired instead of honesty. Is this how nature works Master?"

"People have been nurturing crows' and cuckoos' eggs for a long time," replied the Master.

—The contrast between idealism and the realities of human behavior is beautifully illustrated in this answer.

Yava's question implies that spiritual leaders should remain detached from worldly matters and maintain a singular focus on their spiritual duties alone.

The student's next question, "Is trickery often admired instead of honesty?" implies that the world may not consistently value genuine efforts and honesty. This underscores the contradictory nature of human values, where deceit can be esteemed more highly than sincerity.

The Master's example of the crow and cuckoo further illustrates this point. While the crow diligently builds its nest and cares for its young, embodying qualities of hard work and responsibility, the cuckoo employs a cunning strategy of laying its eggs in the nests of other birds, benefiting from the efforts of others. This example serves as a metaphor for the complexities of human behavior, where both honesty and trickery exist side by side.

Referencing the phenomenon of nurturing crows' and cuckoos' eggs, highlights behaviours that involve deception, which may sometimes be celebrated or valued despite their inherent dishonesty.

In spiritual leadership, it's not enough to only focus on preaching or spiritual tasks. To guide people and understand society better, leaders need to deal with the complexities of human behavior and society as a whole.

31.

Mirror

Yavaa earnestly practiced reciting from memory without looking at the manuscript. Then, he turned towards his Master.

"Master, how does the pages of genius and foolishness reflect?" he inquired.

"A mirror with a quality chemical base will offer a clear reflection of your face. But what will you see in one, without it?" replied the Master.

"Genius is merely the chemical base that reflects your true self," the Master concluded.

—Just as a quality chemical base ensures an accurate reflection in a mirror, geniusness within, acts like a chemical base which enables individuals to showcase their innate talents and intelligence to the fullest extent.

For example, consider a gifted musician who effortlessly composes intricate melodies and captivates audiences with their performances. Their geniusness serves as the foundation that allows their musical talents to shine brightly.

Similarly, geniusness can manifest in various fields, such as science, art, literature, or leadership. It represents the innate potential and brilliance within each person, allowing them to express their unique abilities and insights to the world.

32.

To Gain

"This question has echoed through the ages, Master: 'Nobody understands me,'" Yavaa expressed.

"For those who are acquainted with you, even your back and profile are sufficient to recognize you. But for those unfamiliar with you, even showing them your face won't make you any less of a stranger. This situation fits you as well, Yavaa," the Master explained.

Yavaa sat up, with his back straight, exuding contentment with his newfound understanding.

—The first statement 'nobody understands me', expresses a sense of isolation, unrecognised and misunderstood feelings. True recognition goes beyond surface-level appearances. Those who are deeply acquainted with someone can recognize them even from different angles or without seeing their face.

Additionally, both statements touch upon the complexity of human relationships and the importance of interpersonal connection. Hence one should gain mutual understanding and connection, in order to be understood and recognised.

33.

Becoming

While tending to his goats, the Master heard his student calling out to him. "Flower garden, fruit garden, vegetable garden. In these, does 'garden' refer to the fruits, flowers or vegetables? Without these, what would you consider a 'garden'?"

"Without 'you' which is your self, whatever you become will be meaningless, Yavaa. Without 'you', you cannot become anything," the Master answered.

—The garden alone is just a space that transforms over time, reflecting the ongoing process of cultivation and change. Whereas, the flower, fruit or vegetable act as qualifiers, depicting the self nature of a person. True fulfillment and meaning in life stem from a deep understanding and acceptance of oneself and in shaping one's identity, pursuits, and ultimately, fulfilment in life.

To illustrate this concept, consider individuals who strive for success and recognition in their career without truly understanding their own values, passions, and aspirations. Despite achieving outward success, they may still feel a sense of emptiness or dissatisfaction because their accomplishments are not aligned with their authentic self.

34.

Daily

"Master, crisis always seems to pursue me. I find it difficult to meditate peacefully at any time. I struggle to concentrate on anything, Master," Yavaa confessed.

Master Yavo observed Yavaa with a playful smile and responded with clarity, "Days filled with promise always follow a routine, Yavaa. Aren't you aware of this?"

—Days filled with promise, therefore, often follow a routine because it provides a framework for productivity and growth.

For example, consider a person who implements a morning routine of exercise, meditation and goal-setting. By consistently following this routine, one can cultivate a positive mindset, physical well-being, and clarity of purpose. As a result, each day becomes filled with promise as they work towards their aspirations and experience personal growth.

Additionally, routine can also foster a sense of discipline and accountability, helping individuals stay focused and motivated even when faced with challenges or setbacks.

35.

Goat

As dogs frolicked around the Master, he focused on sorting and serving them chunks of meat.

Yavaa, lost in contemplation, spoke up, "It's incredibly challenging and feels like a constant battle to maintain an unwavering mind. Our minds perpetually think, search, and leap, Master."

"Roaming and getting lost is all a goat understands. What else is there for it to do, Yavaa?" the Master replied.

—The constant activity of the mind, with its thoughts jumping from one thing to another, can be overwhelming for some. The Master's reply taps into psychological concepts about mindfulness and attention. The metaphor of the goat wandering and getting lost suggests a mind that lacks focus and direction, much like how our thoughts can wander aimlessly.

The Master's advice could be seen as a reminder to cultivate mindfulness and awareness, which can help us gain control over our thoughts and emotions.

In essence, the psychology here emphasizes the balance between an active mind and a focused mind. While it's natural for our minds to think and explore, finding ways to ground ourselves and stay present can lead to greater mental clarity and well-being.

36.

Awakening

"My senses are becoming more acute," Yavaa began. "I can discern food being prepared in a distant location. By hearing a cow's cry, I can recount every detail about that particular cow. Even in my deep slumber, I can perceive the color of ants crawling on me. I can distinguish between fifty different types of sweets and even recognize two hundred shades. Isn't this beneficial for me, Master?"

"Which one?" asked the Master.

"My heightened senses..."

"Yavaa, if your ears truly possess sharpness, they can even detect the sounds of waves in a desert. That is true acuity. That is genuine awakening."

—In a desert, where the environment is typically devoid of water and waves, hearing the sound of waves would be considered impossible by conventional standards. Genuine awakening involves this kind of heightened perception, where one can see beyond surface appearances and grasp the deeper truths and interconnectedness of existence.

There is also a scientific theory to the Master's answer. Many deserts around the world were once covered by oceans or large bodies of water. Fossil evidence and geological studies have indicated the presence of ancient rivers, lakes, and marine life in this region. These transformations from oceans to deserts occurred due to tectonic movements, changes in sea levels, and shifts in climate patterns over vast periods of geological time. The remnants of these ancient water bodies can still be found in the form of salt flats, dried-up riverbeds, and fossilized marine life, providing clues to the desert's watery past.

Wise By Birth

"Master, has anyone achieved knowledge and wisdom inherently at birth?" inquired Yavaa.

"Waste transforms into manure.

Coal transforms into a diamond.

There is no birth without a result.

From what I understand, the outcome is not inherent in birth.

It is all one," the Master replied.

—Change is an Universal concept. The outcome is not inherently predetermined or fixed at the moment of birth. Instead, it is influenced by various factors and can evolve over time. All phenomena in the universe are subject to transformation and interconnected in a continuous cycle of change.

38.

Inspiration

Seated next to each other in a dilapidated temple, belonging to a village deity, adorned with dangling, ornamented figures, Master and Yavaa conversed.

Yavaa began to inquire, "The sculpture here is so exquisitely and meticulously crafted. I wonder where the sculptor drew inspiration from. Does creativity define one's uniqueness, Master?"

"The lines traced by smoke are crafted by the work of air, Yavaa," replied the Master.

—Just as the lines of smoke are crafted by the movement of air, an individual's creativity is influenced by various external factors, including cultural influences, personal experiences, and interactions with the world around them. Therefore, creativity is not solely a product of individual genius but is also shaped by external factors beyond one's control.

39.

Cheating / Fraudulence

Yavaa slowly started his conversation, as he savoured the cottonseed milk served by his Master's wife. "Everything is fine, but I find it difficult to forgive certain things, Master."

Observing the children playing outside, Master Yavo gently responded, "To quarrel and reconcile without resolving the conflict to peace, is something only children can manage, Yavaa."

—Thanks to the author for bringing in the traditional age old drink called Paruthi Pal or cottonseed milk, which is popular among the streets of Madurai and various places of Tamil Nadu. It is a mineral -nutrient rich milk, usually served with a dash of cardamom powder, dry ginger powder, pepper powder and jaggery.

Now to the Master's response, it implies that forgiveness involves more than just moving past a conflict; it requires genuine understanding, resolution, and reconciliation. It suggests that true forgiveness involves a deeper process of addressing the underlying issues and working towards genuine peace and harmony.

The words "only children can manage" refers to the innocence of childhood where quarrels are easily forgotten. But it is not possible among elders, who have outgrown their innocence.

40.

Opening

"What is the purpose of our conversations, Master, when the wise suggest that silence is the most effective form of expression?" asked Yavaa.

"To speak, to bite, to eat, to shout, to yawn, to burp—what you do with your mouth depends on the purpose behind it," the Master replied.

—I could read the importance of intentionality and mindfulness in this answer. The actions we do with our mouth, is influenced by the underlying motive or context - whether for communication, sustenance, expression, or bodily functions. Even then, "silence is the best form of expression" suggests that there are moments when words cannot fully convey the depth of emotion or meaning that silence can.

Imagine a couple sitting together on a beach, watching the sunset. As they sit in silence, holding hands, they feel a profound sense of connection and love. The quiet intimacy between them, without uttering a word, speaks volumes, conveying a depth of emotion that words alone cannot capture.

41.

Change

In the midst of a sunny afternoon, parrots joyfully played in the backyard as Yavaa expressed, "Whenever I convey one intention, it is consistently misconstrued in another way, Master." Sulking, he settled down.

"Replace the name of bitter gourd with jackfruit. Then tell me if it is sweet or bitter. Yavaa, lately all your inquiries have been too sour. Either change your palm wine or change your ladle," the Master replied.

—This answer raised a lot of questions within me. Conveying refers to communication. Where does palm wine and its ladle come here? Let's decipher...

The above dialogue reflects a philosophical concept of communication and understanding. The Master's response implies that the way we convey our intentions can be misinterpreted due to the words we use, similar to how replacing the name of a bitter fruit with that of a sweet one changes its perception.

The analogy of changing the palm wine (method of communication) or the ladle (the words used) suggests that altering the approach or choice of words can lead to better understanding and harmony in communication.

In the context of the dialogue, the use of "palm wine" serves as a metaphor for the method or manner of communication. Palm wine is a traditional drink in many cultures, often associated with social gatherings. By mentioning palm wine, the Master is metaphorically referring to the way communication is carried out – it should be done in a manner that is pleasant, enjoyable, and conducive to understanding, much like sharing palm wine among friends. The choice of this metaphor adds cultural richness to the dialogue and reinforces the importance of using an appropriate and pleasant method of communication to convey one's intentions effectively.

42.

Knowledge

"In this pursuit of knowledge, where and when does it culminate, Master? Where's the end to it?" Yavaa asked.

"An empty pot will be filled, and so will a half-filled pot. However, a pot that is already filled can never be filled, just as a pot with cracks can never be filled," the Master replied.

—I would like to narrate a small story here.. a story without a story.

There was a reporter who was very interested in Buddhism. He studied Buddhism for years and considered himself an "expert" on the topic.

One day, he got the chance to fly across the world and meet a real Buddhist monk.

When they sat down, the reporter immediately started telling the monk everything he knew about Buddhism. He went going on and on, acting like he knows everything there was to know. Meanwhile, the monk who remained silent so far, set down down two cups on the table for tea.

As the reporter continued to talk, the monk poured the tea into the glass. the reporter then realised that there is tea pouring all over his legs. The monk continued to pour the tea into the cup, even as it overflowed and poured all over the table and onto the reporter's legs.

Finally, the reporter stopped and asked the monk, "What are you doing?!"

The monk replied, "You can't fill a cup that is already full."

The metaphor of the pot (or cup) suggests that an empty or partially filled mind has the potential to acquire more knowledge and wisdom. However, a mind that is already filled (with I know attitude),

cannot accommodate new knowledge because it is closed off to further learning. Similarly, a mind with inherent flaws or biases, represented by the pot with cracks, cannot effectively absorb new knowledge.

We're all smart. We've all acquired knowledge and have amazing experiences throughout our lives. But still, we must allow ourself to continue to gather new knowledge throughout one's life.

43.

Downfall

Yavaa was particularly weary that day, and Master Yavo observed him silently.

They remained without conversation for some time. Then, the Master began to speak slowly,

"There's something peculiar about the game of ascending a greasy pole. The individual fights with their own body weight, struggling to climb the slippery surface of the pole.

They contend with their rivals as they ascend the slippery pole.

They strive to claim the prize at the top, but for each step gained, they slip back two steps.

Success is determined by their body weight and the strength of their arms.

Regardless, by competing and climbing on the shoulders of others, if they secure the prize, they triumph over others and triumph over themselves simultaneously.

This domain is filled with treacherous slippery poles and slipping poles, Yava."

—Yavaa's silence was clear enough to reflect his worried state of mind. Master, with an intention of motivating him, started talking about the greasy pole game. In many traditions, the greasy pole symbolizes the challenges and obstacles that individuals face in life. In some cultures, participating in the challenge may be seen as a way for individuals to prove their readiness to take on adult responsibilities and face the challenges of the world. The game of ascending a greasy pole often takes place during communal celebrations. It brings people together, fosters a sense of camaraderie, and strengthens social ties within the community.

Thanks to the author for highlighting such traditional themes from our bygone years.

44.

Metabolism

"Is it a new moon night Master? The darkness feels overwhelming." Yavaa queried.

"That's not the point Yavaa. Is the Moon waxing (getting bigger) and waning (getting smaller) or waning and then waxing?" the Master replied.

—We all enjoy watching the moon. But the Master's explanation totally changes our perspective. The Moon goes through both waxing (getting bigger) and waning (getting smaller) phases in its lunar cycle. Philosophically, the waxing or growing phase represents a period of growth, expansion, and accumulation of energy and resources. It symbolizes a time of building momentum, setting intentions, and moving forward with purpose.

Conversely, the waning phase of the Moon represents a period of reflection, release, and renewal. It symbolizes a time for detoxification, shedding old habits, and making space for new growth and transformation.

By embracing both phases of the lunar cycle and understanding their parallels with metabolism, individuals can cultivate a holistic approach to well-being, nurturing their bodies, minds, and souls in harmony with the rhythms of the natural world.

45.

Life Time

Master Yavo observed Yavaa gradually drawing nearer from a distance.

"What must one do to gain an extended life time Master?"

Master promptly responded, as if expecting the question, "That, too, is a method. Delay all your aspirations." he said.

—The Master's advice can be found in many recent Zen texts. He says to live longer and happier:

1. Don't be too focused on achieving things all the time because it can lead to stress and dissatisfaction.

2. Pay attention to the present moment instead of always thinking about the future. Being mindful and appreciating what you have right now can bring more peace and fulfillment.

3. Instead of constantly chasing after success or material possessions, learn to be content with what you have. This attitude can lead to a more satisfying and possibly longer life.

46.

Flower

"The nights overturn, and the days fully blossom. Have you observed this, Yavaa?"

"What do you mean, Master?"

"Nature, that it is, Yavaa."

—Nature and its cyclical patterns are filled with motivation for humans. However, we often fail to recognize it. Periods of darkness (nights) are followed by periods of brightness and growth (days). Seasons change, tides ebb and flow, and life follows a rhythm of birth, growth, decline, and regeneration.

Just as nature follows its course with grace and balance, individuals can learn to navigate life's ups and downs with greater wisdom and harmony.

47.

Dual

"Master, how can we distinguish between knowledge and intelligence?" Yavaa inquired.

"cattle waste that does not transform into Gorochana, cacti that don't yield agar, (a fragrant product) deer that doesn't produce a yellow pigment for cosmetics, and knowledge that doesn't impart wisdom— these are all the same, Yavaa.

Before said knowledge becomes understanding, wisdom lies in practicing what you comprehend."

—There is a difference between possessing information (knowledge) and truly understanding its significance and application (wisdom). The above given examples show a potential for transformation or utility. Similarly, possessing knowledge without gaining understanding, practicing and applying what one understands, renders it ineffective or incomplete.

48.

To Know

With a serious gaze fixed at a distance, Yavaa searched intently, mouth slightly agape. "Is it feasible to comprehend anything thoroughly, Master?" he inquired.

"Engagement is the initial stride toward understanding. A carpenter doesn't pay attention to the fruits or leaves. Their focus lies solely on scrutinizing the nature of the tree."

—Comprehending anything thoroughly may not always be easy. In the initial stages, whether it's a subject, concept or problem, our focus remains only on the surface level, according to our desires. However, by adopting a carpenter-like approach, one can delve deeper into the subject, gaining a clearer and more comprehensive understanding.

49.

Corpse

Master Yavo was engrossed in crafting a seat from a log, using a wooden scraper.

"Women embody universal power, don't they, Master?" Yavaa queried.

"They say, Yavaa, there was a time when man and woman coexisted in the same body. If that were the case, creation would've been out of control". Master continued, "Human population would have skyrocketed across the globe. Other creatures would've perished. Eventually, even humankind," the Master explained.

The student immediately asked, "How do we define a Man, Master?"

"They are storage cells, Yava, just storage," the Master burst out in laughter.

—The idea that there was a time when men and women existed in the same body is just a story, not something we know to be true. It can even symbolize the idea of balance and integration of masculine and feminine energies, within an individual. In our society, men and women have different roles and functions, which helps keep things organized. For example, child birth, which helps control how many people there are in the world. So, having different gender roles helps keep things balanced.

The title Corpse for this chapter may suggest a metaphorical death of an old paradigm or a concept, giving rise to new possibilities or understanding.

50.

Animal Instinct

On a day when Master was battling a severe cough and consuming a blend of black pepper, betel leaf, and honey, he remarked,

"Those who stand apart crave the company of the crowd . Yet, those lost in the crowd yearn for solitude. Such is the way for certain individuals. Amidst a crowd, one may feel isolation, while in solitude, one may sense the weight of a crowd. We are creatures of habit, Yava."

— The chapter begins with our age-old preparation of a concoction for cold and flu. Perhaps the Master had isolated himself for a couple of days due to his poor health condition and expressed his feelings of loneliness with his student, Yavaa.

We constantly battle between our innate desire for connection and our need for individuality. Additionally, all these behaviors and experiences are often governed by habitual patterns, suggesting a deeper exploration of the psychological and societal forces at play in shaping human behavior.

51.

Expectation

"Yavaa, do we experience anything without even utilizing it?"

"No, Master. We utilize buffaloes for their milk, trees for the fruit they bear, and much more, all solely for their benefits."

"Indeed, Yavaa. Think over this: Monkeys devoid of skills, are never raised by humans."

—Humans tend to engage with and invest in beings or activities that offer some form of utility or benefit. Therefore, humans are unlikely to invest time, effort, or resources into raising or caring for anything, that do not possess skills deemed beneficial or desirable. There is always an underlying expectation.

52.

Whirlpool

While basking in the salty breeze on the seashore, student Yavaa posed his query, "Master, this world is in perpetual spinning motion. Does it align with time or our memories?"

"Yavaa, time signifies a positive spin, whereas memories signify a negative spin."

—Time is typically viewed as a forward-moving force, symbolizing progress, growth, and opportunity. It offers the potential for new experiences, accomplishments, and positive changes. In this sense, time signifies a positive spin.

On the other hand, memories are often tied to the past and can evoke emotions associated with regret, sadness, or longing. Even happy memories can sometimes evoke a sense of melancholy, as they remind individuals of fleeting moments or lost opportunities. Thus, the world always aligns with the positive spin, which is time.

53.

Contradicts

"Just like nature, our life too, brims with contradictions, wouldn't you agree, Yavaa?"

"Certainly, Master. Yet, we fail to understand it during our young age."

"Youth lacks maturity, while maturity often lacks youthfulness," saying so, Master laughed out heartily.

—While youth brings the excitement of new possibilities and the freedom to explore, it can also be marked by impulsiveness and naivety. On the other hand, maturity offers the benefits of wisdom and perspective gained from life experiences, but may come with a sense of rigidity or complacency.

Both youth and maturity have their own strengths and weaknesses, and individuals may navigate through life seeking upon the best qualities of each stage of life to enrich their personal growth and development.

54.

This and That

"Sadness resides within every happiness,

Happiness within every sadness.

Memories of sadness become droning bees,

Memories of happiness become soothing feathers for the ears.

Such is the essence, Yavaa. It's nature."

—"Memories of sadness turn into droning bees" Like the constant buzzing of bees, memories of sadness may linger and weigh heavily in our minds.

"Memories of happiness become soothing feathers for the ears" Happy memories are portrayed as gentle and calming, offering reassurance and relief from the burdens of sorrow.

It emphasizes the cyclical and interconnected relationship between happiness and sadness, illustrating how each informs and shapes the other, ultimately contributing to the rich tapestry of human existence.

55.

Respective Nature

"When a cloth is torn, it's called a rag.

A net has holes as well. What do you call it, Yavaa?"

—Perception plays a significant role in shaping our understanding and evaluation of the world around us. It encourages a shift in perspective to recognize the inherent value or potential within objects or situations, even when they may contain imperfections or flaws.

56.

Path

"What will our impressions be like,
Master?"

"Rows for ants,

Herd for a young sheep,

Path for an elephant,

Respective powers reflect respective paths.

Whether a single path or an impression,

are you one among the row, path, or impression, Yavaa?"

—Each creature's journey is shaped by its unique traits and strengths.

The passage invites contemplation on the diversity of paths that individuals may take in life and encourages embracing one's unique strengths and abilities to chart a fulfilling journey.

57.

Question

Master applied pan chuna on a betel leaf before handing one to his student, who enjoyed it as well.

"The five elements of Earth truly amaze me, Master. Their collaborative nature is both intricate and fascinating," the student remarked...

"Water extinguishes fire, while the combination of air and water gives rise to waves. Fire always ascends, whereas water descends. Below us lies the land, surrounded by air in all directions. Above us and everywhere is the sky," the student explained in awe.

"When sky and water unite, they pour down as rain, saturating the soil. Fire, sand, water, air, and sky come together to form this pot," isn't it Master ?"

"Yes, Yavaa. This pot will eventually break, but it will never truly disappear. It will transform into something else. These pots are a product of our craftsmanship, Yavaa. It's in our nature to mold the unbaked ones together," the Master concluded.

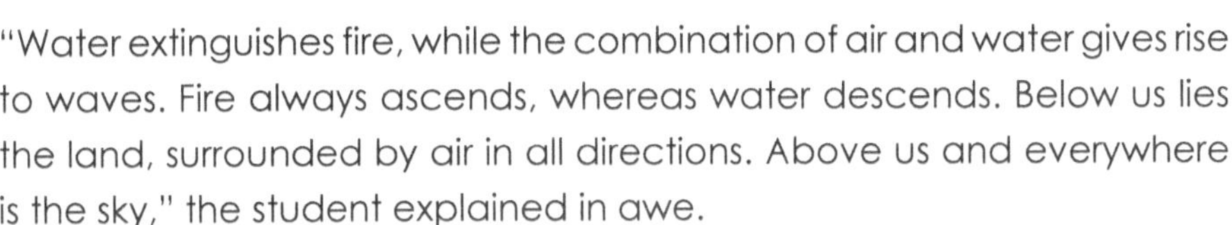

—By referring to the pot as a product of craftsmanship and stating that it is human nature to mold the unbaked ones together, the Master underscores the role of human creativity and intervention in shaping the world around them. This suggests a deeper connection between humans and the natural world, where they actively participate in the ongoing process of creation and transformation.

Overall, the philosophy conveyed in this passage celebrates the interconnectedness of all things and emphasizes the inevitability of change and transformation.

Greed

"Yavaa, today I have a question for you," the Master announced.

"Yes, Master," Yavaa replied.

"Are there any prerequisites for aspiring or desiring something?" the Master inquired.

"Can the water we envision in our dreams truly quench our thirst, Master?" Yavaa questioned.

"Excellent," responded Master Yavo.

—Desires, even if vividly imagined or longed for, may not necessarily fulfil one's true needs or satisfy the underlying longing. Just as the water in dreams may seem refreshing but ultimately fails to quench physical thirst, desires may sometimes lead to disappointment if they do not align with deeper or genuine needs.

We must have an understanding of what truly nourishes our soul. Otherwise it simply turns into greed.

59.

Cause and Deed

"Master, is it possible for actions to go against our intentions?" asked Yavaa.

"A poison administered to end a life can also be used to save one.
Similarly, a medicine intended to heal can also bring about death. Yes, such occurrences are indeed possible," the Master affirmed.

"Why does this paradox exist, Master?" inquired Yavaa.

"What is contained within the pot can only be served with a ladle, Yavaa," replied the Master.

—This exchange illustrates a philosophical concept often referred to as the principle of double effect. One same substance (represented by the pot) can have different effects depending on how it is used (served with a ladle). This paradox highlights the complexity of moral decision-making and the interconnectedness of actions and consequences.

60.

Deed or Cause

"Master, which comes first, the deed or the cause?" asked Yavaa.

"It's not as straightforward as we may initially perceive, Yavaa. First, a deed transpires, and only then does its underlying cause become apparent. Are you not familiar with this concept?" the Master explained.

"I'm having difficulty grasping it, Master," Yavaa admitted.

"Are you aware of the story of a king, who sustained an injury on his fingers and narrowly escaped death? That's the case Yavaa," the Master replied.

—According to this perspective, deeds occur first, and it's only through their consequences that the underlying causes become clear.

Master emphasises that the deed (i.e., the observable behavior or event) precedes the understanding of its cause. This highlights the psychological tendency for individuals to interpret events based on their observable outcomes, rather than objectively analyzing the underlying causes or motivations.

It encourages individuals to question their assumptions and beliefs, and to adopt a more objective perspective when interpreting the actions and events around them.

61.

Equilibrium

While Master plucked 'Gandhari' chillies from the plant, he conversed with his disciple Yavaa.

"There exists no scale to evenly weigh happiness and sadness. To maintain equilibrium between the two is what we refer to as emptiness," he explained.

—Gandhari Chilli otherwise known as Birds Eye chilli, is a small sized, high spice variety It has antifungal and microbial qualities, increases appetite, speeds up metabolism.

The idea of "emptiness" arises when one strives to maintain equilibrium between the two states of happiness and sadness. This concept aligns with certain philosophical perspectives, particularly in Buddhism, where the pursuit of equanimity is central.

62.

Writings and Speech

"People tend to hold written documents in higher regard and trust them more than verbal communication, Master," the disciple remarked.

"Men inherently distrust anyone, Yavaa. We were the ones who relied on pigeons instead of parrots for sending messages," the Master recalled.

—Distrust in communication is not a new phenomenon and is deeply ingrained in human nature. It suggests that skepticism towards both written and verbal communication is a fundamental aspect of human behaviour.

The comparison between pigeons and parrots symbolizes the preference for written communication over verbal communication. Written documents, being tangible and permanent, are often perceived as more reliable and trustworthy compared to verbal communication, which can be more prone to error or misinterpretation.

63.

Benefit

"What is the point of creating thorny plants?" Yavaa grumbled, extracting a thorn that had pricked his foot.

"Fur for a rabbit, a moustache for cats, a tail for a squirrel, and a mane for a lion. do you believe all these serve merely aesthetic/beauty purposes Yava? By pricking you, it spreads or gets planted itself elsewhere," the Master explained.

—Every creation bears important functional roles in their survival, navigation, communication, and social interactions within their respective ecosystems. The passage emphasizes the idea that in nature, traits often have multiple benefits beyond mere aesthetics.

64.

Ancestral

"When does a person despise or worry about their inherent adaptability, Master? Regardless of the circumstances under which one flourishes, will each individual's yearning never be fulfilled?" Yavaa questioned.

"There exists a disparity between preference and compulsion, akin to the difference between a king and a slave, Yavaa. The dogs incessantly hound after their lost untamed, wild nature driven by consensus. Are you familiar with this, Yavaa?" the Master inquired.

—The conflict between what individuals do and what they feel they have to do, is equal to comparing a king (who is free to do as he pleases), and a slave (who is controlled by others). The mention of dogs longing for their wild nature suggests that many individuals feel a desire to be true to themselves, but societal expectations hold them back.

The answer explores the tension between personal fulfillment and conforming to society's expectations, which has been there for ages now.

65.

Confusion

"What do unanswered questions teach us, Master?" Yavaa asked.

"I will tell you what Buddha said, Yavaa. A question that originates from a clear mind always holds the answer," the Master explained.

—Questions that originate from a clear mind are those that arise naturally, without the interference of confusion or clutter. Similarly, when the mind is free from distractions and biases, individuals are better equipped to recognize and understand the answers to their questions.

Truth - An Experiment

"Is one who scrutinizes himself and imposes self-punishment considered righteous, Master?" Yavaa inquired.

"He has realised the truth that by acknowledging his errors, mistakes can become holy, Yavaa," the Master affirmed.

—Mistakes become holy when they are approached with humility, wisdom, and a sincere commitment to self-improvement and spiritual growth. We must realise the transformative power of acknowledging and learning from mistakes, leading to personal growth and spiritual enlightenment.

67.

Season

Enduring a feverish night beneath the leaky roof of his hut, Yavaa received a concoction prepared and served by Master Yavo.

"Wealth in youth is akin to rain for sowing seeds, while wealth in old age resembles rain that destroys harvest," Master Yavo remarked.

—Tamil poetess Avvaiyar rightly said, Poverty in youth and wealth in infirm old age, will always be miserable. Wealth received during inappropriate stages can never be enjoyed.

In youth, when one is energetic and has time ahead, wealth serves as a resource for investing (planting seeds) for future growth and prosperity. In old age, when one's energy and opportunities for future growth may be more limited, wealth becomes a burden.

Just as rain is essential while sowing seeds but destroys during harvesting, wealth plays different roles at different stages of life.

68.

Where and What?

The village temple's chariot festival was in full swing, filled with grandeur and spectacle. Both the Master and the student observed from afar, reveling in the scene.

"Master, the dilemma of where to search for what perplexes me greatly," the student remarked.

"Looking for a question within a crowd and seeking an answer during moments of solitude is always wise Yavaa," Master Yavo replied.

—Master Yava teaches us the best strategic approach to problem-solving skills in this answer.

Being wise means finding a balance between listening to others and thinking over by yourself. When with a group of people, we get different ideas, which can help us think creatively and come up with new questions or thoughts. But sometimes, it's important to take time alone to really focus and think deeply without any distractions. This quiet time lets us concentrate and explore on our ideas more deeply. By switching between being around others and being alone, we can make the most of our thinking abilities and find better solutions to problems.

69.

Feelings

"Man is a peculiar creature, having numerous causes for tears, laughter, and brooding," observed the student.

"It's a matter of the disparity in time and location," explained Master Yavo.

"Rocks and trees remain unaffected by variations in time and place. They lack the capacity for vindictiveness. They neither sulk nor smile," the Master elucidated.

—Different times in one's life can evoke different emotions based on past memories, present circumstances, and future expectations. Similarly, different locations can influence emotions based on factors such as familiarity, comfort, or cultural significance. Overall, mention of time and location by Master Yavo indicates that these external factors play a significant role in shaping human experiences and emotional responses.

On the other hand, rocks and trees are static entities that do not change over time or respond to their environment in the same way humans do. Rocks and trees do not possess intentions or emotions, such as spitefulness or revenge, that are associated with vindictiveness. Hence, our emotions are a big part of what makes us human.

70.

Toddy

Yavaa ambled along unsteadily, stumbling around, with a slurry voice, expressing his thoughts and relishing the moment.

Master Yavo's tone turned serious as he questioned, "Why isn't there a bottle to seal away sorrow and uncork joy, Yavaa?"

—The student's emotional state, particularly the presence of sorrow and the desire for joy, is being demonstrated here. Emotions cannot be easily controlled or suppressed, much like trying to contain them in a bottle. Attempting to escape or suppress them through alcohol or other means is ultimately futile.

Let us acknowledge the nature of emotions and embrace them with courage and acceptance, rather than seeking temporary relief through external means.

71.

Co-Passenger

"What qualifications are necessary for preaching, Master? Is it knowledge, education, experience, wisdom, practice, or awareness? Which one, Master?" inquired the student.

"A tree, a wheel, a pair of feet are sufficient, Yavaa. If you attempt to comprehend it straightforwardly and superficially, you can never preach to anyone," the Master explained.

—The connection between a tree, a pair of feet, and a wheel in the context of preaching can be understood as follows:

A tree represents strength, growth, and rootedness. In preaching, it symbolizes stability, resilience, and the ability to stand firm in one's beliefs.

A pair of feet symbolizes movement, journey, and progress. In preaching, it represents the preacher's willingness to embark on a journey of learning, exploration, and sharing.

A wheel symbolizes motion, change, and continuity. In preaching, it signifies the cyclical nature of life, adaptation to change, and ongoing learning and growth.

Overall, these symbols suggest that preaching is not confined to specific locations, objects, or individuals. Instead, it is a dynamic and universal practice that draws upon strength, movement, and continuity inherent in life.

72.

Example

Engrossed in cutting bamboo to craft baskets, both Master and student conversed.

"How would you define a youthful heart, Master?" inquired Yavaa.

"It's akin to a fox tied upon to a lion's back, Yavaa," replied the Master.

"Does the lion symbolize the body or the mind?" questioned Yavaa.

"Does the fox represent your body or your mind?" the Master countered.

—The metaphor of a fox tied to a lion's back represents the juxtaposition of two contrasting qualities: the agility and cunningness of the fox with the strength and nobility of the lion. By asking whether the fox represents the body or mind, the Master prompts Yava to consider how he perceives his own identity and the relationship between his physical and mental aspects.

1. Fox: The fox is known for its playfulness, curiosity, and creativity. It symbolizes the youthful spirit.

2. Lion: The lion, on the other hand, is a symbol of strength, courage, and nobility. In the metaphor, the lion symbolizes maturity, wisdom, and inner strength.

This dialogue explores the complex relationship between the body and mind, highlighting their interconnectedness and the influence they have on each other. It means having the cleverness and energy of a fox, along with the strength and dignity of a lion. This combination makes for a lively and balanced approach to a youthful life.

73.

Promise

In the late afternoon, Yavaa labored to gather tamarinds from the tree, feeling both exhausted and full. Suddenly, he began to shout.

"Master, I had committed to gather tamarind from ten trees to the farm owner before sunset," Yavaa exclaimed.

Master Yavo smiled and remarked, "Not just fishes, Yavaa, even men can find themselves caught or trapped in net. And remember, it's called a 'promise.'"

—Comparing a promise to a fish caught in a net shows how breaking a promise can make someone feel stuck, just like a fish trapped in a net. This makes them feel guilty or regretful, similar to how a fish can't swim freely when it's caught. The metaphor reminds us that making a promise is a big responsibility. Just like a fisherman needs to be careful not to catch unintended fish, people should be careful when making promises to avoid hurting others. Overall, it shows that keeping promises is important for building trust and keeping relationships strong.

74.

Dependence

Master and Yavaa proceeded cautiously, navigating a long wooden plank over the lake. Suddenly, Yavaa posed a question.

"Master, do justice and injustice receive identical judgment? Some scriptures seem to suggest so!" he inquired.

"It is a great offence to curtail or condense the two different sides together as one. To the right or to the left, safeguard your footing to maintain balance Yavaa. Do not lean towards either side" advised the Master.

—The Master's response to Yavaa's question about justice and injustice receiving identical judgment can be likened to crossing a plank above a lake.

"Curtail or condense the two different sides together " suggests that attempting to restrict or constrain opposing forces can lead to negative consequences.

"Maintain balance" means finding an equilibrium that allows for flexibility and adaptability while avoiding extremes.

"Safeguard your footing" suggests being mindful of one's position or stance in a situation and ensuring stability and security.

"Do not lean towards either side" warns against leaning too far towards either extreme. It encourages maintaining impartiality, objectivity, and fairness in decision-making and actions.

Overall, the philosophy conveyed in the statement emphasizes the importance of balance, moderation, and impartiality in navigating life's challenges.

75.

Right Time

"How should one speak and when should one speak? How can I learn this, Master?" inquired Yavaa.

"Adopt the mouth of a turtle, holding on to a stick, carried away with the beak of a flying crane. That's the formula, Yavaa," replied the Master.

—The Master in his answer recollects a fairy tale, "The Turtle and the Crane,". A turtle once, faces a dilemma when its pond dries up in the summer. The crane, wanting to help its friend, suggests a plan to relocate to a new home. The crane proposes that the turtle bite onto one end of a sturdy stick with its mouth and hold on tight until they safely reach their destination, cautioning the turtle not to open its mouth during the flight.

As they soar through the sky, the villagers spot the unusual sight of a flying turtle and shout in astonishment. Filled with pride and wanting to respond to the villagers' cheers, the turtle opens its mouth. Tragically, it loses its grip on the stick and falls onto a hard rock, resulting in its demise.

The moral of the story emphasizes the importance of self-control and mindfulness. It teaches us that reacting impulsively to external situations, especially out of pride or vanity, can lead to unfortunate consequences. Instead, it is wiser to remain calm, think before speaking or acting, and maintain self-awareness at all times.

In this story, the crane represents patience. With their long, slender beaks, cranes use precision and grace, patiently waiting for the right moment to catch a fish. This aspect symbolizes speaking with clarity and choosing words carefully, advocating for caution in communication and avoiding hasty speech.

76.

Closeness

Master sat calmly, releasing wisps of smoke, while relaxing on his cement bench.

"Master, what is the safest place in this world, and what is considered the most dangerous place?" inquired Yavaa.

"The space that lies between a mother and a father. That is also the most treacherous too, Yavaa," the Master replied.

—Referring to the space between a mother and a father can be seen as a "twin-edged weapon". The closeness with parents can provide a sense of security, stability, and emotional support for children. However, if this space is overly sheltered or devoid of challenges, it may inhibit children's growth and development. Growth often occurs through facing and overcoming obstacles, learning to navigate conflicts, and developing resilience in the face of adversity.

Allowing children to experience some degree of autonomy and independence enables them to develop essential life skills, and cultivate a sense of identity and agency.

77.

Self

"I've got this specifically for you," stated the student Yavaa, presenting a pot of freshly made toddy to his Master.

"Ah, wonderful!" exclaimed the Master joyfully, savoring his drink and indicating for Yavaa to ask his questions.

"In reality, what is individuality, Master?" inquired Yavaa.

"It's a dye that remains unfading and unyielding to the rain, Yavaa," the Master explained.

—individuality is something intrinsic and inherent to a person, much like a dye permeates and colors fabric. Just as a dye does not wash away in the rain, genuine individuality persists despite adversity or pressures to conform.

Individuality is the distinct essence of each person, representing their true self and the ability to remain authentic despite facing life's challenges.

78.

To Evaporate

"What initiates the flow of tears, Master?" asked the student.

"Sun - the senses,

Sea - the minerals.

When they combine, it pours down as rain (tears), Yavaa," the Master explained.

—The sun, sea, and rain to convey a deeper philosophical message.

The sun represents our senses for emotional upliftment.

The sea represents the cause to stir up human senses.

When the sun and sea combine, they form rain, which represents tears. Rain symbolizes the manifestation of emotions, both positive and negative, that result from the interplay of external stimuli (sun) and internal experiences (sea).

The Master subtly highlights the importance of minerals in the human body. Minerals play a key role in regulating our senses, significantly influencing our health. Any imbalance in mineral levels like salt or potassium, can lead to health issues, symbolized by "tears."

Reconciliation

Yavaa stood silently observing the trail of ants for quite some time. Suddenly struck by a thought, he leaped up with a question, "Master, is it advisable to adapt to every situation?"

"Is it wise for a fox to cease its howling in times of need?" the Master responded.

—Fox is considered a clever animal with a keen sense. Howling is often associated with alerting others or expressing distress. By suggesting that the fox ceases its howling implies that, sometimes it's necessary to adapt or modify one's behavior in response to the demands of a situation.

While it's essential to remain true to oneself and one's principles, there are times when it may be necessary to adjust or adapt in order to navigate challenges effectively or achieve desired outcomes.

80.

Difference

"Master, is it beneficial for sages to associate with ordinary folks?" inquired Yavaa.

"Those who fail to discern or realise the distinction are not truly sages, Yavaa. Engaging with the public is one thing, assimilating with them is another," the Master explained.

—It's important to talk to others, share what we know, and join in social activities. This means communicating, working together, and sharing ideas. But assimilation is different—it's about becoming too much like everyone else, adopting their beliefs and ways of doing things.

As a sage, it is always good to talk and share wisdom, but he should also stay true to his belief system and values. In common, any person shouldn't change too much to fit in with others. Finding a good balance between being part of a group and staying true to ourselves keeps our wisdom and authenticity intact.

81.

Movement

Yavaa, while casting stones into a water pond and observing the resulting ripples, turned to his Master.

"Master, is our mind akin to the pond, the stone, or the ripples?" he inquired.

"Temptation characterizes the nature of the mind.

The stone represents the external element,

Ripples signify our thoughts.

However, questions are akin to sharp knives, Yavaa.

Remove the rust from your blade," the Master advised.

—In this, metaphorical imagery to illustrate the nature of the mind and the role of questioning is depicted. Our minds are often tempted by desires, impulses, and distractions, making it hard to stay focused and clear.

External influences, like a stone thrown into a pond, can stir up our thoughts and emotions, causing disturbances in our minds.

These thoughts are like ripples on the pond, created by the impact of external influences.

"Removing rust from your blade" implies the importance of sharpening our questioning skills and maintaining clarity in our inquiries.

Asking questions helps us uncover deeper truths and gain understanding.

82.

Crime

"Who is the criminal here? Who is not the criminal here? Is fault found in those with a guilty conscience? Are those without guilt, law-abiding?" questioned Yavaa.

"The guilt of the guilty,

The guilt of the innocent, both prevail Yavaa.

Those who don't embrace guilt,

those who do embrace guilt, both exist, Yavaa," the Master elucidated.

—This sounds like guilt is inevitable.

One might feel bad or guilty about what they've done. This guilt can come from knowing what's right and wrong or from what society expects. People who haven't broken any rules can still feel guilty. This feeling comes from their conscience, which cautions them to do the right thing.

Some people accept their guilt and try to make things right, while others ignore or deny it, pretending they haven't done anything wrong.

Guilt can have varying psychological impacts, influencing self-esteem, relationships, and mental health. Understanding and managing guilt is a complex process that involves introspection, self-awareness, and sometimes, forgiveness.

83.

Sin

Yavaa had chosen to spend the day with his Master, resulting in a slower pace of his questioning.

"Master, what deed is more heinous than killing?" he inquired.

Letting out a long breath, the Master replied, "To strip or erase out innocence from a child, Yavaa."

—A Childs innocence carries fundamental sense of trust, safety, and joy in the world. While death is a tragic loss, the loss of innocence can have lasting psychological and emotional consequences that deeply affect a child's well-being and development.

Preciousness of childhood innocence and the responsibility adults have, to protect and nurture them, is clearly emphasised here.

84.

Depth

"How does one comprehend the depth of silence, Master?" asked Yavaa.

"Listen attentively to the space between each wave and the next.
Pause your ears during the intervals between each bell toll. That is silence. Silence is merely the trickery of sounds, my child," the Master explained.

—Silence can have various psychological effects, ranging from relaxation and calmness to feelings of discomfort or unease. The term "trickery" implies deception or manipulation. Silence may deceive us into thinking that there are are no sounds, when faint or imperceptible sounds may still be present. The act of pausing and listening attentively to silence can promote mindfulness and present-moment awareness. Just as light and darkness enhance each other's qualities, silence and sound complement and enrich each other.

85.

Need

Amidst heavy rains and overflowing rivers, Master and Yavaa sought cover beneath taro leaves, attempting to shield themselves from the downpour while running.

In the midst of thunder, Yavaa posed a question, to which Master Yavo replied, "In the midst of an overflowing river, what use is a small cup, Yavaa? In a place where there is no sunlight, shade becomes a luxury."

—Taro leaves are the large, heart-shaped leaves of the taro plant (Colocasia esculenta). They are commonly used in cooking and are a staple ingredient in many cuisines, particularly in tropical regions. Taro leaves are known for their mild flavor and are often used in dishes such as soups, stews, curries, and wraps. They are rich in nutrients and are a good source of vitamins, minerals, and dietary fiber.

Now coming to the Master's statement, amidst an overflowing river, a small cup symbolizes something insignificant or inadequate.

It emphasizes the futility of attempting to make a difference.

Conversely, in a location where there is no sunlight, shade becomes a valuable commodity. Shade provides relief from the harshness of the environment and becomes a luxury.

The Master's response about the "small cup" and "shade becoming a luxury" emphasizes the relative value of resources based on context. In a situation like an overflowing river or absence of sunlight, even something as simple as a taro leaf can become invaluable for protection and comfort.

86.

Path Way

"It's either long hair or a clean shave. Quite peculiar, Yavaa.

One has it shaved,

Another has it long,

I keep a tuft only at the center.

The middle path is always preferable, Yavaa," the Master remarked.

—Long hair and a clean shave represent opposite ends of a spectrum. Long hair symbolizes a more traditional or natural appearance, while a clean shave represents a more modern or groomed look.

The Master's mention of keeping a tuft only at the center suggests a balanced approach between the two extremes.

Opting for the middle path emphasises the importance of maintaining a balance between modernity and tradition. It represents flexibility, open-mindedness, and the ability to embrace the best of both worlds.

87.

One and Two

"One signifies darkness,

Darkness marks the beginning.

Two represents the flow of events,

Two embodies the universal melody."

—I can see a lot of significance here.

One represents the start of things, like the beginning of a story. It's like when things are unknown or mysterious, before anything else happens. It's also like how darkness comes before daylight, marking the start of a new day.

Two stands for having two sides or forces that balance each other out. Yin and Yang, conscious and unconscious, day and night, good and evil, rational and emotional. Two or duality reflects the interplay of opposites and the potential for harmony, balance, and growth through integration. They combine as melody in music.

88.

Three and Four

"The music of three is surplus,

Three always signifies abundance.

Four doesn't solely represent scriptures,

Without four, there would be no differentiation."

—This chapter beautifully explains the importance of numbers three and four. The saying "three always signifies abundance" means that the number three often represents having lots of something.

In nature and in human-made things, we often see groups of three. For instance,

there are three main colours (red, blue and yellow),

three dimensions (length, breadth, width), and

three phases of matter (solid, liquid, gas).

In numerology, three is seen as bringing creativity, communication, and growth.

Number four is important for categorizing and organizing things.

We use the four cardinal directions (north, south, east, west) to navigate,

we divide the year into four seasons (spring, summer, autumn, winter).

While the number four is important in religious texts (the four Vedas), it's also used in other areas like math and science. It helps us see patterns and organize information.

89.

Five and Six

"The outcome of five is life,

Perceiving all five is wisdom.

Though every one is aware of all six,

Six is everlasting."

—Now let us see the importance of the next two numbers - five and six.

The number five is often associated with life and vitality. Humans have five senses (sight, hearing, taste, touch, smell), which are essential for experiencing and interacting with the world. In this context, perceiving all five may refer to being aware of and using their potential aptly, will help us gain wisdom.

Number six holds enduring significance or qualities that transcend time. Apart from the basic five senses, the concept of sixth sense includes the mind or consciousness as the sixth sense. This could symbolize the holistic nature of perception and awareness.

The number six represents six tastes—sweet, sour, salty, bitter, pungent, and astringent—which are fundamental to the human experience of food and flavor. As per these aspects, six becomes everlasting.

Seven and Eight

In seven, the world aligns,

In seven, the mind defines.

In eight, our yearning merges,

In eight, paths converge.

—Number seven holds significance in both external and internal realms.

There are seven days in a week,

seven ragas,

seven colors in the rainbow, and

seven continents on Earth.

This repetition of the number seven in various contexts can lead to cognitive associations and patterns, allowing the mind to define and interpret the world around it.

"In eight, our yearning merges, In eight, paths converge" refers to the 'Ashta' or eight directions, (north, south, east, west, northeast, southeast, southwest, and northwest). There is a convergence or meeting point of all these directions.

91.

Nine and Ten

Nine paths, an illusion,

All nine is reflected on our face.

If all Ten don't vanish, what is hunger then.

—Number nine depicts Navarasa means the nine emotions in Indian art. Calling Navarasa an illusion means these emotions are not permanent. They come and go, influenced by different events and thoughts. And all these nine are reflected on our face.

Hunger makes all Ten vanish. What are those ten? Honour, Caste, Education, Valor, Knowledge, Charity, Penance, Endeavor, Laziness and Lust. Real hunger makes us forget everything; none of those ten can compare themselves or withstand before the real power of hunger.

92.

Burden

On a long, highway road, the Master and his disciple journeyed, passing stone pillars shouldering heavy burdens. Master Yavo mused,

"To the bearer,

feather and fence seem alike,

Fur and slingshot seem alike."

—This comparison holds a significance. The bearer, in this context, represents a neutral or passive observer who lacks the ability or inclination to differentiate between objects based on their attributes or functions. Psychologically, this could suggest a lack of discrimination.

Both are seemingly disparate objects. A feather is light, delicate, and typically associated with flight or freedom. While a fence is solid, sturdy and used to set boundary thereby restricting freedom.

Likewise, fur and a slingshot are typically considered distinct objects with different properties and uses. Fur is soft, warm and often associated to protect animals. A slingshot is a tool used for launching projectiles, which at times is used to harm animals.

In simple terms, the statement means that the bearer sees things as similar, even if they're different by nature. Regardless of whether objects have positive or negative properties, the bearer treats them similarly, indicating a neutral or indifferent attitude.

93.

Thoughts

Having finished his daily exercise, the Master stood drenched in sweat. Yavaa sat in silence, lost in contemplation, until he unexpectedly inquired,

"Thoughts, like fire, endure, ceaselessly scorching me."

"Why do you ignite, Yavaa?"

"Do I possess a choice?"

"Thoughts resemble fire, indeed. Yet, you behave akin to an oil well, igniting it further. Transform into a well of water."

"How do I function as a well?"

"Unleash the springs from within."

—Thoughts can be intense, consuming, and potentially destructive if left unchecked. At times, our behaviour is likened to an oil well, helping it spread rapidly.

Water is associated with calmness, purity, and tranquility. By becoming a "well of water," the character is encouraged to cultivate a sense of inner peace, serenity, and emotional balance.

By accessing these internal springs, they can nurture a sense of calmness and equanimity, effectively quenching the flames of intense thoughts and emotions.

94.

Creation

Within the cave, the Master and Yavaa stood quietly, observing the paintings adorning its walls.

Tracing his fingers over one, the Master remarked,

"A pregnant woman and a lactating woman, possess two bellies, yet for an artist, it's perpetually two lives and half a belly."

—The author has wonderfully captured this statement with figurative language, comparing the experiences of a pregnant woman, a lactating woman, and an artist.

In ancient Tamil dialect, words such as Suli and Pali are used to denote a pregnant woman (suli) and a lactating woman (pali). Both these are described to have "two bellies", which means, both these women have to eat food to nourish themselves and their babies.

From the artist's perspective, a woman's body represents "two lives and half a belly." "Two lives" underscores both the mother's life and that of her unborn or nursing child, highlighting the profound duality of motherhood and the intimate bond between mother and child. In this context, the artist sees a similar connection with the artwork he is creating.

The term "half a belly" symbolizes the physical transformations a woman experiences during pregnancy or lactation. While this might appear to be a mere observation of bodily changes, from the artist's viewpoint, it signifies his own transformative journey. Just as a mother nurtures life within her, the artist nurtures his creation, striving to bring his painting to its fullest expression and beauty.

95.

Path

Amid gathering medicinal herbs in the forest, Yavaa inquired,

"What purpose do values serve in our lives now, Master?"

"A horse without reins,

Palm juice without calcium,

A flag without a rope,

All equal in essence, Yavaa."

—Let's start to relate these examples with the purpose of values:

A horse without reins can't be controlled or directed properly. It's like not having values to guide our actions and decisions, which can leave us feeling lost or unsure about what to do.

Palm juice mixed with calcium is good for health, acting as a refreshing drink. But without calcium, it turns into toddy, an alcoholic drink. This shows how adding values in our lives can make a big difference, just like having calcium in palm juice, which makes it healthier.

A flag without a rope can't be raised or flown, losing its purpose. Similarly, without values to support our beliefs and ideals, our efforts and character might not soar high like a flag.

Just like certain things need their essential parts to work properly, we need values, to lead a complete and meaningful life.

96.

Sentence

Exhausted from engaging in silambattam, Master Yavo confessed,

"I have journeyed with you for many years Master. I am gradually approaching your path. Impart wisdom for me, Master."

"Not solely for you, Yavaa, but for us,

We are the dust, Yavaa. Dust of this vast Universe.

As they rise up in the air, they then descend gracefully."

—Interconnectedness and shared humanity between the master and the student is reflected in this answer.

By referring to both of them as "the dust of this vast Universe," the Master suggests that they are both equal and interconnected parts of the universe. This implies that the wisdom imparted by the Master is not solely for Yava's benefit but is also relevant and meaningful for the Master himself. It underscores the idea that they are on a shared journey of learning and growth, united by their shared existence within the greater cosmos.

Pain

Student Yavaa was serving his monthly routine of Amavasya lunch at his home. Yavaa and his Master Yavo dined on palm leaf plates.

"Have these trials or difficulties persisted since ancient times, Master?"

"Hmm... do you know of the hardships chronicled by earlier writers in scriptures, Yavaa?"

"No, Master."

"Hunger... Are you familiar with the other contemporary challenges, Yavaa?... Disease."

Yavaa sat quietly, immersed in contemplation for an extended duration.

—Societies may have made advancements in some areas, yet, certain fundamental challenges remain constant throughout history. Hunger and disease were the most contemporary challenges, and these difficulties continue to affect people, till the present day.

This perspective encourages reflection on the universality of human experiences and the importance of addressing enduring issues for the well-being of individuals and communities.

98.

World

Conversations about ancient Tamil texts persisted on that day.

"The world is an extension of what, Master?"

"Wind and fire, offspring of the sky,

Blue and water, mother and father,

This world is a fusion of five illusions,

All this has been previously stated, Yavaa."

—The world and its connectivity to natural forces is explained here.

The passage describes the natural elements of wind, fire, blue (sky), and water in metaphorical terms, attributing familial relationships to them. It suggests that wind and fire are like children of the sky, while blue (representing the sky) and water are like parents. This imagery symbolizes the interconnectedness of these elements and their importance in the world.

The passage encourages thinking about how natural elements are connected, what reality truly is, and how our understanding of these concepts has persisted over time. It prompts us to explore these ideas to better understand the world and our role in it.

Five Illusions refer to our senses—like seeing, hearing, touching, tasting, and smelling—that shape how we understand things.

99.

Indicator

Amidst the swirling dusty wind, Yavaa and his Master conversed, seated on their customary bench outside.

"When and for what will this mind ponder, Master? It remains a perplexing enigma."

"The frog's croak, the dragonfly's low flight, the eagle's wing drying, ants scaling a wall, a stroke priming its brush, a rat burrowing a hole, strokes and cranes heading north, winged white ants fluttering about, termites unearthing their anthill, observing the circles of Sun and Moon— all these are indications of rain, Yavaa...

There isn't any indicator for our mind."

—It is interesting to learn about the various natural phenomena that serve as indicators or omens of rain, such as the frog's croak, the dragonfly's low flight, and the behavior of different animals.

However, unlike the observable behaviors of animals and insects, there are no explicit signs or omens that can reliably predict the state of the human mind.

This observation highlights the complexity and unpredictability of human emotions and thoughts. The human mind operates in a more nuanced and enigmatic manner, often defying easy explanation or prediction.

100.

Love

Master Yavo was happily playing with his neighbour's child.

"The world is entirely immersed in joy,

Saints always contemplate sorrow..."

"Just as separating fish from its spines and consuming it, separate happiness, Yavaa.

Recognizing that it will eventually yield sorrow, we still long happiness.

Happiness within sorrow and sorrow within happiness is intrinsic. Nothing exists in isolation, Yavaa...

It's all interconnected."

—There's a lot of happiness in the world. Even then, wise people like saints often think about sadness. They understand that life has both good and bad parts, so they don't ignore the sad things.

The Master compares happiness and sadness to a fish and its spines. They're connected, and you can't have one without the other.

People sometimes try really hard to be happy all the time, even if it's not realistic. Hence, trying too hard to be happy can lead to disappointment when things don't go as planned. Loving both sides helps us understand life better.

Colour of Water is White

During the wintry season, enveloped in dense fog, unable to discern each other's faces, Yavaa and Master Yavo sat in silence. Lost in thought, Yavaa uttered,

"When will one's true self be unveiled, Master?"

"In states of boiling and freezing, we can know one's essence, Yavaa.

I acquired this insight from water."

—Water exhibits distinct behaviors when subjected to extreme temperatures. When heated, it boils and turns into vapor, while when cooled, it freezes and becomes solid ice.

Its ability to change forms depending on temperature, reveals its adaptability and responsiveness to external conditions, as well as its versatility and resilience.

Just as water reveals its essence through changes in temperature, observing how a person reacts in challenging or extreme situations can provide insight into their character and true colors.

102.

Goal and Carelessness

Beside the swirling and gushing waters, as Yavaa collected sand, growing weary, he inquired,

"Who can attain their objective, Master?"

"A deaf frog always reaches its goal, Yavaa. It heeds neither the good nor the bad."

—Frogs rely heavily on their sense of hearing to detect danger or locate prey, but a deaf frog would not be swayed by sounds or distractions around it. By remaining single-minded and undeterred by external distractions or circumstances, individuals can increase their chances of success in reaching their objectives.

103.

Patience

Arriving at a mountain spring to refresh themselves, the Master and student settled in. To alleviate his body heat, Master Yavo submerged his foot in the water.

"What must I do to validate my worth?" inquired Yavaa.

"To whom?"

"To myself."

"You refer to your abilities?"

"Regardless of the aspect."

"Are you prepared to walk on water?"

"Yes."

"Wait until it freezes."

—Student Yava, in an eagerness to prove his capabilities and gain recognition, starts a conversation with his Master. The Master suggests that achieving something extraordinary, like walking on water, represents proving worth. But at the same time, Master advises Yava to wait until the water freezes before attempting to walk on it.

Even to prove our exceptional achievements, we need to realise the importance of patience and the right time.

104.

Gravity

As Student Yavaa dried chunks of tapioca on a rock, a question arose within him.

"Master, how does a magnet attract iron?"

"Does the magnet pull the iron or does the iron pull the magnet towards itself?" master Yavo responded, countering Yavaa with a question.

—Dried tapioca chunks, made from a starchy root vegetable, are very useful. They can be:

1. Rehydrated and added to dishes like soups, stews, or desserts.
2. Eaten as a snack, sometimes flavored or seasoned (known as tapioca chips).
3. Ground into flour for baking or used to give texture and flavor to recipes.
4. Used to thicken sauces, gravies, or puddings when added to liquids.

Regarding the student's question about magnets and iron, it's like a back-and-forth. The magnet pulls the iron, but the iron also responds by moving towards the magnet. Symbolically, it represents a broader theme of the dynamic interplay between different forces in the universe, the complexity of relationships, or the interconnectedness of opposites.

105.

Burden

Yavaa arrived with a big smile on his face, brimming with happiness.

Master Yavo watched him with interest.

"We are all like donkeys...

Is the thing you're carrying just dirt,

or does it hold precious things?

You will understand Yavaa."

—People are compared to donkeys carrying loads. The load could represent various things in life, such as responsibilities, burdens, or experiences. Merely dirt represents mundane or trivial matters and precious things symbolises valuable experiences, knowledge, and opportunities. It will also take time for us to determine whether our happiness we truly carry is worth it or not.

106.

Complete

"How would you describe yourself, Master?"

"The term 'I' is either the quotient or division of our dreams, Yavaa," Master replied.

—Who you are can be the question or answer of your dreams and ambition. Individual identity is the result of dividing or separating our dreams, desires, and aspirations. Each part contributes to shaping our identity, beliefs, and goals. Therefore, the term "I" represents the culmination of our dreams and ambitions, divided into various aspects that define who we are as individuals.

107.

Way

Master was busy tending to his fields, clearing unwanted plants.

Just then, Master Yavo noticed crabs and rats scuttling about.

One crab lay lifeless under the sun. Master Yavo paused, observing it for a while.

Restless, he sat wearily on the boundary, his mind beginning to waver. "When a spear passes from the rectum to the mouth, which path does life take to leave us?"

He sat in silence, his mind restless with thoughts.

—During 13th century, Impalement, a brutal form of torture and execution was in practice. The line "spear passing from the rectum to the mouth" is a reference to this impalement. It involves piercing a person's body with objects like stakes, poles, or spears often penetrating from the rectum, partially or entirely. It was commonly employed as a punishment for "crimes against the state" and was considered an extremely severe form of capital punishment in many cultures.

The question about which path life takes to leave us is not about actual physical paths but rather about the mystery of death. It's like asking where life goes after we die, which is something we don't fully understand.

Overall, it's a deep question that makes us think about the meaning of life and what happens after death.

108.

Listen

"Where do you belong Master?"

"Everywhere."

"Who are your loved ones Master?"

"Everyone."

"What's your approach?"

"Uniform for all."

"What's your name Master?"

"My path is my name, dear Yavaa"

"..... I have no one" Yavaa spoke, tears welling in his eyes.

—In this final dialogue between the Master and his student Yavaa, they share their true identities. Master responds with a sense of universality saying, he belongs everywhere, loves everyone, and approaches all situations uniformly, reflecting compassion for all beings. When asked about his name, he associates it with his life philosophy or spiritual journey rather than a conventional name.

However, Yavaa's response contrasts with the Master's inclusive outlook. Yavaa expresses a feeling of isolation and emotional emptiness. His statement "I have no one" suggests a deep sense of loneliness and disconnection. The tears in his eyes indicate the depth of his emotional pain and longing for companionship and belonging.

The Master's name Ya-Vo symbolises 'yaavum ondru' in Tamil, which means, one who considers everything the same. The student's name Ya-Vaa symbolises 'yaavum atravan' in Tamil, which means, one who has no one.

Express your reflections:

Express your reflections:

Express your reflections:

Express your reflections: